Get the Ball!

Written by
Rob Waring and **Maurice Jamall**

Before You Read

to fall

to score a goal

to kick

to push

to run

bags

blue team

red team

referee

score

soccer

surprised

win

Jenny

Kerry

Alex

Anthony

"I want the Blues to win," says Jenny. She is talking to her friend Kerry.

Today there is a big soccer game. The Reds are playing the Blues.

Kerry and Jenny are watching the game.

Kerry likes the Reds and Jenny likes the Blues.

Jenny's boyfriend Alex plays for the Blues.
Kerry likes Anthony. He plays for the Reds.
"Come on, the Blues," says Jenny. She wants the Blues to win.
"Come on, the Reds," says Kerry.

It is a good game. Everybody
wants the ball.
Alex is a good player. He takes
the ball from Anthony.
"Alex is very good," says Jenny.
"He's okay," says Kerry. She
does not like the Blues.

Alex has the ball. He kicks it at the Reds' goal.
Alex scores a goal for the Blues!
The score is 1–0 to the Blues.
Jenny says, "Good goal, Alex!"
Kerry says nothing. Kerry is not happy.

Anthony gets the ball, but Alex pushes him. Alex takes the ball.

The referee sees Alex.

"Hey!" says Anthony.

Kerry says, "Hey! Stop that, Alex."

Jenny says, "Good play, Alex!"

Anthony has the ball. He runs to the Blues' goal. Anthony scores a goal for the Reds!
"Good goal, Anthony!" says Kerry. Kerry is very happy.
Now the score is the Reds 1, the Blues 1.
But Jenny says nothing. Now she is not happy.

Alex looks at Anthony. He wants the Blues to win.
Anthony wants the Reds to win.
The two teams are having a good game.
"Come on, Anthony!" says Kerry. "Come on, the Reds."
"Come on, the Blues!" says Jenny. "Come on, Alex."

Anthony has the ball. He is running to the Blues goal.
Alex pushes Anthony. He takes the ball from Anthony.
"Hey!" says Kerry.
Anthony is angry with Alex. Anthony is a good player,
but he is not playing well now.
"Come on, Alex!" says Jenny.

Alex and Anthony run for the ball. But Alex kicks
Anthony and takes the ball.
"Ouch!" says Anthony. "Don't do that!"
Anthony is very angry with Alex now.
"Don't kick me!" he says.

Anthony is angry with Alex. He gets the ball
and kicks it away.
"Get the ball, Anthony," says Alex.
"No!" says Anthony.
Alex says, "Get the ball, Anthony!"
"No!" says Anthony. He is very angry with Alex.
"You get the ball, Alex!"

Anthony watches Alex get the ball.
But Anthony starts running. He runs at Alex.
Alex thinks, "Why is Anthony running at me?
What's he doing?"
Anthony says, "No, Alex. No!"

Anthony runs at Alex. "Alex!" he says.
Alex thinks, "Why is Anthony running at me?"
Anthony pushes Alex. Alex falls down. He is very surprised.
Alex says, "Hey! Anthony, what are you doing? Don't do that!"

"Look!" says Anthony.

"Look at what?" asks Alex. Some bags fall on the ball.
Anthony shows Alex the bags. "Look . . . the bags!
See!" says Anthony.

"Wow, Umm . . . Thanks!" says Alex.

"That's okay," says Anthony.

Everybody runs to Anthony and Alex. They are very happy with Anthony.

"Alex! Alex, are you okay?" asks Jenny.

"I'm okay, thanks. Thanks, Anthony," says Alex.

"You're a good friend. Let's play soccer."